Baik Speaks Korean

Ryder Shava

Rosen
REAL
READERS

Rosen
Classroom
New York

This is my friend Baik. Baik is **Korean American**. He was born in Korea and now lives in the United States.

Baik lives in San Francisco, California. California is more than 5,000 miles away from Korea.

Korea is in **East Asia.** Korea is made up of the countries of North Korea and South Korea. Baik is from South Korea.

Baik tells me about South Korea and teaches me some Korean words. He shows me the South Korean **flag**. Baik says the Korean word for "flag" is *gitbal.*

Baik lived in a city called Seoul. Seoul is the **capital** of South Korea. Baik says that the Korean word for "city" is *doshi*.

Baik tells me about his family. This is Baik's mom. Her name is Ji-wan. Baik says *eomma* means "mom" in Korean.

Baik's dad's name is Jihoon. Baik says that *appa* means "dad" in Korean.

Baik has an older brother named Woojin. Baik says that *hyong* means "brother" in Korean.

Baik likes to play soccer. He says
chuggu means "soccer" in Korean.

Baik and I have fun together. He is my friend. Baik says *chingu* means "friend" in Korean.

Glossary

capital   The most important city of a country or state.

East Asia   The eastern part of the Asian continent.

flag   A piece of cloth with a design that is the symbol of a country.

Korean American   An American who was born in Korea.